Stamina Training

for Teen Athletes
Exercises to Take Your Game to the Next Level

by Shane Frederick

Consultant:
Thomas Inkrott
Head Strength and Conditioning Coach
Minnesota State University, Mankato

CAPSTONE PRESS
a capstone imprint

Sports Illustrated Kids Sports Training Zone is published by Capstone Press,
1710 Roe Crest Drive, North Mankato, Minnesota, 56003.
www.capstonepress.com

Library of Congress Cataloging-in-Publication Data
Frederick, Shane.
  Stamina training for teen athletes : exercises to take your game to the next level / by Shane Frederick.
    p. cm.—(Sports illustrated kids. Sports training zone.)
  Includes bibliographical references and index.
  ISBN 978-1-4296-7679-3 (library binding)
  ISBN 978-1-4296-8001-1 (paperback)
  1. Teenage athletes—Training of—Juvenile literature. 2. Endurance sports—Juvenile literature.
I. Title. II. Series.
  GV711.5.F735 2012
  613.711—dc22   2011033559

Editorial Credits
Anthony Wacholtz, editor; Heidi Thompson, designer; Eric Gohl, media researcher;
    Marcy Morin, scheduler; Laura Manthe, production specialist

Photo Credits
Capstone Studio: TJ Thoraldson Digital Photography, all interior training photos

iStockphoto: Prokhorov, design element (backgrounds); Newscom: Icon SMI/Jeanine Leech,
35; Sports Illustrated: Al Tielemans, cover (bottom middle left), 45, Bill Frakes, cover (top),
8, Bob Rosato, 15, David E. Klutho, cover (bottom left), John Biever, cover (bottom middle
right), 9, 27, John W. McDonough, 5, Manny Millan, 11, Peter Read Miller, cover (bottom
right), 7, 10, Simon Bruty, cover (bottom middle), back cover, 6, 14, 44

Printed in the United States of America in North Mankato, Minnesota.
102011   006405CGS12

TABLE of CONTENTS

WHAT IS
Stamina
Training?

The game clock is counting down the final seconds. The next point wins the volleyball match. The finish line is in sight. Are you still at your best?

When you play sports, you want to be as strong at the end of your game, match, or race as you are at the beginning. In other words, you want stamina. You want endurance.

This book will show you some ways you can improve your overall endurance, no matter what you're training for. Even if you're not practicing for a specific sport, the exercises should be fun. They're also a good way to get some of the regular exercise you need each day.

Are You Ready?

Before you begin training, ask yourself the following questions: Is your body ready for stamina training? What are you training for? What muscles do you need to use and how will you be using them? Are you strong enough? Are you in shape? If you are new to exercising and training, make sure you start slowly. Don't do too much too soon!

Before you begin any of these exercises, it's important to warm up. Get your blood

pumping and your heart beating a little harder. Do a set of jumping jacks and go for a light run or jog in place. Do this for about 10 minutes. Now you're ready for your workout.

When your drills are done, be sure to spend a few minutes cooling down. Jog, walk, and stretch your muscles.

EXERCISES ARE OFTEN DONE IN SETS, WITH A NUMBER OF **REPETITIONS**, OR REPS, IN EACH SET. BE SURE TO PACE YOURSELF BY RESTING FOR ONE OR TWO MINUTES BETWEEN EACH SET.

FACT: Be sure to include a proper warm-up and cool-down for your workout.
- Warm-up: 10–15 minutes
- Stamina train: 20–30 minutes
- Cool-down: 10–15 minutes

U.S. OLYMPIC VOLLEYBALL PLAYER LOGAN TOM

REPETITIONS—THE NUMBER OF TIMES AN EXERCISE IS DONE

Form Your Foundation

Whether you're preparing for endurance sports, team sports, or racket sports such as tennis, make sure you have a base level of **aerobic** fitness. You might have to strengthen your heart and lungs before you start your training. Your muscle fibers need to use the oxygen from blood pumping through your body.

Some ways you can build up your aerobic fitness include:

- walking
- jogging/running
- bicycling
- using elliptical machines
- stair climbing/stair climbing machines
- performing aerobics/calisthenics

NORWEGIAN CROSS COUNTRY SKIER MARIT BJOERGEN

As you do these workouts, your heart and lungs will get stronger. Before long you will see your endurance start to improve.

FACT: When you exercise you lose fluids that your body needs. Be sure to hydrate and replenish that liquid by drinking water or a sports drink before, during, and after your workout. Don't wait until you're thirsty.

Heart Rate Monitor

To achieve a proper level of aerobic fitness, you don't want your heart to be set on overdrive. You want your heart beating 65 to 75 percent of its maximum heart rate. Anything more than that and your body stops using the oxygen supplied by the heart. Then your workout changes to anaerobic exercise.

You can use a heart rate monitor to gauge your heart rate during your workout. Some treadmills, stationary bikes, and elliptical machines have them. You can also wear one.

To find your optimal heart rate for aerobic fitness, subtract your age from 220 then multiply that number by 0.65. Then multiply that same number by 0.75.

AEROBIC—WITH OXYGEN
ANAEROBIC—WITHOUT OXYGEN

Endurance Sports

There are two kinds of stamina in sports. The first refers to endurance sports, such as distance running, swimming, bicycling, cross-country skiing, canoeing, and kayaking. Endurance sports also include multisports, such as triathlons.

The other kind of stamina refers to an athlete's ability to last a whole game or a whole season. This type of stamina is used in football, basketball, soccer, lacrosse, and hockey.

Running Form

- Don't look at your feet. Keep your eyes on the road, track, or trail in front of you.
- Keep an upright posture. Looking up will help keep your neck and back straight.
- Keep your shoulders low and loose.
- Keep your arms loose but avoid over-swinging.
- Don't overstride. Your feet should land under your body, not out in front of you.

U.S. OLYMPIC GOLD MEDAL RUNNER ALLYSON FELIX

Focus on Technique

When it comes to improving stamina for endurance sports, the best training is the activity itself—running, cycling, swimming. But stamina requires **efficiency**. You need to focus on your technique.

If you're a swimmer, make sure your strokes and kicks are smooth and strong. If you're a cyclist, you should be comfortable on your bike. You may need to adjust the seat or handlebars if your posture makes you sore.

EFFICIENCY—GETTING THE MOST OUT OF A WORKOUT WITH THE LEAST AMOUNT OF ENERGY USED

Going the Distance

Ready, set, go! Whether you're thinking about trying out for the cross-country team or want to run to get in shape, it's a good idea to set a goal for yourself. You could start with a five-kilometer (5K) fun run. If you're an experienced runner, a 10K or a half marathon (about 13 miles) might be in your future. Maybe your goal is to run for a half hour without stopping to walk.

No matter the goal, you have to build up your running endurance. That will take commitment, dedication, and patience. You can't become a marathon runner overnight!

In order to prevent injuries, make sure you start slowly and gradually build your running distances. If you're trying to build distance, go for one long run per week. As you push toward your goal, increase your running distances in small increments—about 5 percent each week.

U.S. MARATHON RUNNER
MEB KEFLEZIGHI

Use a Calendar

To help you organize your training, go online to find a calendar so you can track your progress. Most running schedules are set up for seven- or eight-week periods with a race day being the ultimate prize. There are many calendars to choose from depending on your goal, your running experience, and your time. Find one that suits you best.

INTERVAL TRAINING
20–30 MINUTES

The best kind of training you can do for endurance sports is the sport itself. But you need to do more than run, bike, or swim in order to improve your stamina. Devote one or more days of your weekly workouts to **interval** training. Intervals—also called speed work—increase your aerobic fitness. You will get more out of the long workouts built into your schedule.

WHAT YOU'LL NEED

• track

1. After a proper warm-up, run 200 meters at 70 percent intensity.

INTERVAL—THE SPACE OR TIME BETWEEN TWO POINTS

2. Walk for two minutes or until your breathing and heart rate return to normal.

TIP: You may not have access to a track or you may prefer doing intervals on a bike. If that's the case, pick spots on your route, such as mailboxes, electrical poles, or an intersection. Then sprint or ride hard to those points.

3. Run 400 meters at 60 percent intensity.

4. Walk for two minutes or until your breathing and heart rate return to normal.

5. Repeat the 200s and 400s, with walking time between each run. Start with three to four reps at a time. Then build up to six to 10 reps over time.

VARIATION

To add some difficulty to the workout, do your intervals in an area with a slight incline.

Legs, Feet, and Hips

During the 2010 World Cup in South Africa, the United States' Landon Donovan scored a historic goal. He became a hero to U.S. soccer, launching Team USA into the knockout round of the biggest soccer tournament on the planet. Donovan's goal in the 1-0 victory over Algeria came after more than 90 minutes of play.

Donovan sprinted up the pitch with his teammates and passed ahead. The Algerian goalkeeper stopped a shot by Clint Dempsey but couldn't secure the ball. Donovan won the race to the loose ball and booted it into the net, sending his teammates and soccer fans into a frenzy.

It takes excellent soccer skills to score goals like Donovan. But it also requires great fitness and endurance. That's true for athletes in all sports. Football and lacrosse players need strong legs throughout their long games. Basketball players need energy in the fourth quarter to defend on a fast break or take a game-winning jump shot.

MLS STAR
LANDON DONOVAN

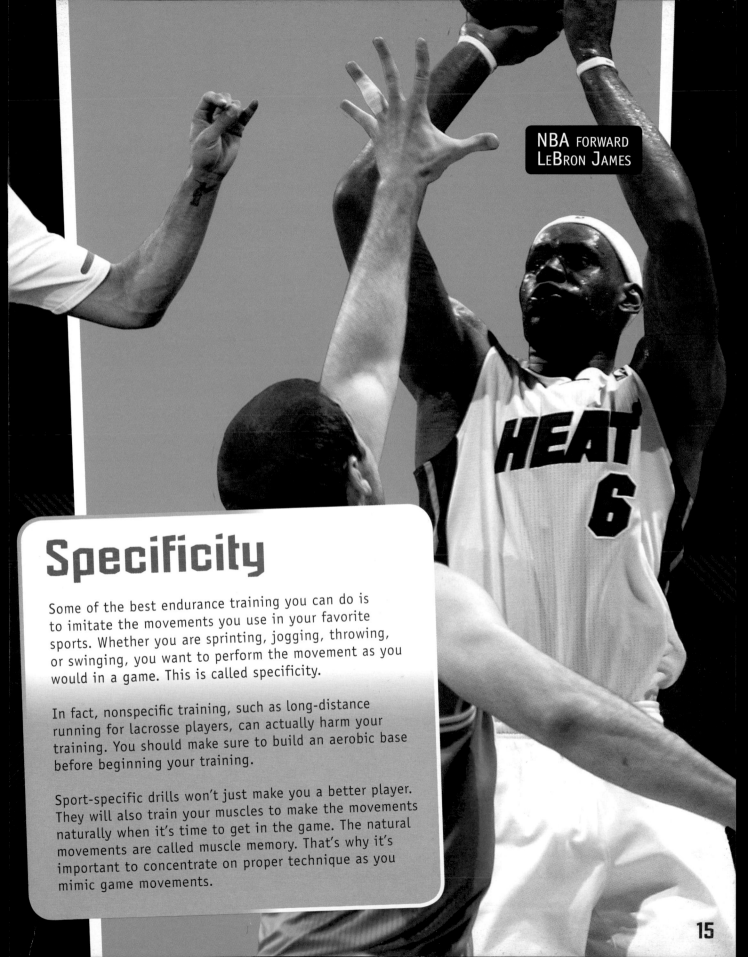

Specificity

Some of the best endurance training you can do is to imitate the movements you use in your favorite sports. Whether you are sprinting, jogging, throwing, or swinging, you want to perform the movement as you would in a game. This is called specificity.

In fact, nonspecific training, such as long-distance running for lacrosse players, can actually harm your training. You should make sure to build an aerobic base before beginning your training.

Sport-specific drills won't just make you a better player. They will also train your muscles to make the movements naturally when it's time to get in the game. The natural movements are called muscle memory. That's why it's important to concentrate on proper technique as you mimic game movements.

FARTLEKS

20–30 MINUTES

In many sports the action rarely stops. Players run all over soccer and lacrosse fields at various speeds. Athletes need the ability to sprint and recover quickly so they can sprint again. One way to prepare for that is by fartlek training. Fartlek is a Swedish word meaning "speed play." Just like playing soccer and lacrosse, you'll be moving without stopping over a long period of time.

WHAT YOU'LL NEED

• enough space to run various speeds, such as a track

1. After you warm up, jog for 60 seconds.

Cross Training

No matter what sport you're training for, don't limit yourself to just that activity. Cross training and participating in other sports have many benefits. Cross training helps prevent injuries from overusing muscles, improves overall fitness, and provides a break from your routine so you stay motivated.

Mix in strength or flexibility training or go for a walk or a hike. If you're a runner, go for a bike ride or a swim. Play some soccer or pick-up basketball with friends.

Even if you choose to focus on one activity, be sure to change things up. Avoid doing the same routine over and over. Run different routes and pick out several bike trails to check out.

2. Run hard at 80 percent for 90 seconds.

3. Jog for 45 seconds.

4. Sprint at full speed for 10 seconds.

5. Jog for 30 seconds.

TIP:

As your endurance improves, add more intense sprints and backward running to the workout. But don't eliminate your jogs and walks—those are important for recovery.

6. Walk for 30 seconds.

7. Run hard for 60 seconds.

8. Repeat steps 2 through 7 three or four times.

KILLERS

20–30 MINUTES

If you stop by a basketball practice, you might see players running back and forth on the court. Is the coach punishing them for poor play with this tough drill? Not necessarily. What they're doing is similar to the running you see during a game. They're running up and down the floor, sprinting in short bursts, and changing direction. If you're still moving fast at the end of these "killers," you'll be moving fast at the end of the big game.

WHAT YOU'LL NEED

• basketball court

1. Start on the baseline of a basketball court.

2. Run to the closest free-throw line and run back.

3. Run to the half-court line and run back.

4. Run to the far free-throw line and run back.

5. Run to the far baseline and run back.

VARIATION

ADD SOME VARIETY WITH OTHER MOVES FROM YOUR SPORT. BASKETBALL PLAYERS CAN ADD BACKPEDALING AND SIDEWAYS SHUFFLING IN A DEFENSIVE STANCE TO PARTS OF THE EXERCISE. TENNIS PLAYERS CAN DO THEIR SPRINTS ON A TENNIS COURT OR A SMALLER AREA.

VERTICAL JUMP

3 SETS OF 10 REPS

Endurance in your legs isn't just about being able to run late in games. You have to jump in many sports too. **Plyometrics** are a great way to build stamina in the muscles you use for jumping and hopping. Working on your explosiveness can give you the stamina to make a big spike or block at the volleyball net or put back an offensive rebound in a basketball game.

1. Stand with your feet shoulder-width apart.

2. Bend your knees and swing both arms back.

PLYOMETRICS—HIGH-INTENSITY WORKOUTS THAT FOCUS ON EXPLOSIVE MUSCLE MOVEMENTS; THEY OFTEN INCLUDE SETS OF HOPS, LEAPS, JUMPS, AND BURSTS

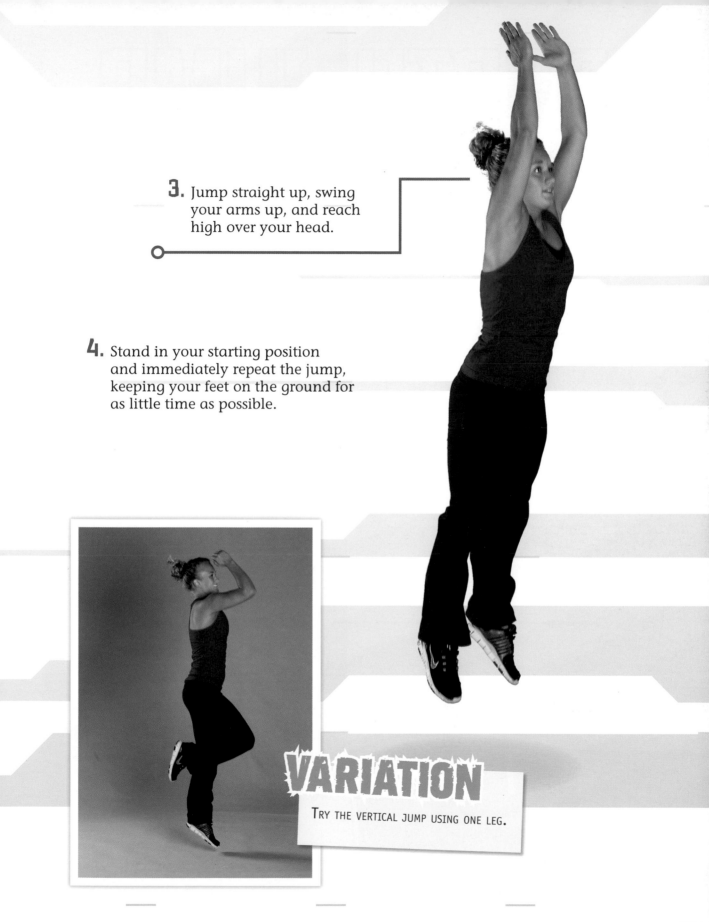

3. Jump straight up, swing your arms up, and reach high over your head.

4. Stand in your starting position and immediately repeat the jump, keeping your feet on the ground for as little time as possible.

VARIATION

Try the vertical jump using one leg.

DEPTH JUMP

Wide receivers make quick cuts on the football field to beat a defender. Hockey players change directions and skate past opposing players. When you play sports that require quick, powerful movements such as jumping and cutting, you have to train your muscles properly. Similar to vertical jumps, depth jumps are a plyometric exercise. They work fibers in your muscles that fire with speed and explosive power.

WHAT YOU'LL NEED

• exercise box

1. Stand on the edge of an exercise box.

2. Step off the box. Don't jump!

TIP:
Wear comfortable, proper-fitting athletic shoes that help absorb some of the shock from the jumps.

3. Land on both feet.

Immediately jump straight up as high as you can, reaching high over your head.

5. Turn around, step back on the box, and repeat.

JUMP ROPE

3 SETS OF 10 REPS

When athletes grow tired and lose stamina, they often stop moving their feet. This can be a big disadvantage in competition. If basketball players are caught flat-footed trying to play defense, they might get beat to the basket. A shortstop might be one step short of reaching a hard-hit grounder. Jumping rope is a good way to build stamina and keep you moving.

WHAT YOU'LL NEED

• jump rope

EXERCISE 1: Two-leg jump: Jump with both feet.

EXERCISE 2: One-leg jump: Jump with one foot lifted slightly behind you.

EXERCISE 3: High knees: Run in place, bringing your knees up as high as possible.

EXERCISE 4: Double jump: Jump twice in one full swing of the jump rope.

Work-to-Rest Ratio

Athletes work hard during games, but they need to rest too. Hockey players skate in shifts of 45 to 60 seconds. Then they rest on the bench for a couple of minutes before going on the ice again. Football players go hard from the snap for 10 to 15 seconds before getting about 30 seconds of rest. Volleyball rallies last five to 15 seconds with the same amount of time for a break before the next serve.

When you play your sport, think about how you move. Are you constantly moving? Are you getting time to rest? Your workouts should involve movements similar to what you do in a game. Your work-to-rest ratio should follow a similar pattern.

Strong **Arms** and **Chest**

Detroit Tigers pitcher Justin Verlander threw his second career no-hitter in 2011. To go the distance, he had to be as good late in the game as he was in the first inning. The way Verlander was pitching that day against Toronto, the Blue Jays hitters didn't have a chance. With two outs in the ninth inning, Verlander was trying to get the final out and make history. He went into his windup and threw a fastball to Rajai Davis. The pitch hit 100 miles per hour on the speed gun! By the end of the game, Verlander had thrown 108 pitches.

Baseball pitchers often show signs of **fatigue** late in games. As their arms get tired, the ball's **velocity** slows down or the pitchers have trouble hitting the strike zone. It's why relievers and closers often replace them for the final innings. Fatigue is part of the game. But as athletes train, their goal is to build stamina so they can overcome fatigue late in games—just like Verlander.

Tennis players want to hit a blazing ace in a five-set match. Volleyball players want the ability to spike kills if they end up in the fifth set. In football, quarterbacks need upper-body endurance to make strong, accurate throws in the fourth quarter. The linemen who protect him use their hands and arms to block defenders more than 60 times per game. The idea is the same for all athletes who use their upper body.

FATIGUE—STATE OF BEING VERY TIRED
VELOCITY—MEASURE OF AN OBJECT'S SPEED AND DIRECTION

MLB PITCHER
JUSTIN VERLANDER

MEDICINE BALL CHEST PASS

3 SETS OF 10-20 REPS

Many sports require players to throw a ball. One way to improve endurance and be effective with your throws is to work with a heavier ball. A medicine ball can do the trick. A medicine ball chest pass is a plyometric exercise similar to passes made on the basketball court. It's also a good drill for football linemen who push their arms out to block.

WHAT YOU'LL NEED

- medicine ball
- solid wall

1. Stand three to four feet away from the wall. Stand with your feet shoulder-width apart and your knees slightly bent. Hold the ball in front of your chest with both hands.

2. Fire the ball against the wall at eye-level.

3. Catch the rebound. Allow the ball to come to your chest.

4. Pass the ball again. Try to go as fast as possible. Avoid pausing between passes.

VARIATION

TRY THIS EXERCISE WITH A PARTNER. STAND FOUR TO FIVE FEET APART AND PASS THE MEDICINE BALL BACK AND FORTH.

CHEST PRESS
WITH RESISTANCE BANDS

3 SETS OF 10-12 REPS

There are dozens of exercises you can do with **elastic** resistance bands or rubber cords. The bands are often used in physical therapy sessions to treat injuries. But they are also good for training specific body parts, such as the arms and chest. Many athletes, including swimmers, gymnasts, and football players, use them to build strength and endurance.

WHAT YOU'LL NEED

- floor mat (optional)
- secure, sturdy object, such as a fence post or a pole

1. Wrap the resistance band around a sturdy object behind you at chest level. Place one end of the band in each hand.

2. Start with your elbows bent at 90-degree angles and your forearms parallel to the floor. Make sure there is no slack in the band.

3. Push your arms straight out, keeping them parallel to the ground.

4. Bring your arms back to the original position.

VARIATION

INSTEAD OF PRESSING OUT WITH BOTH ARMS, ALTERNATE ARMS. START BY PUSHING WITH YOUR LEFT ARM, AND THEN PUSH WITH YOUR RIGHT.

TIP:

Resistance bands come in varying degrees of resistance, from easy to difficult. Start small and increase the tension as you get stronger.

ELASTIC—ABLE TO CHANGE BY STRETCHING OR SQUEEZING AND RETURN TO ORIGINAL SHAPE

OVERHEAD PRESS
WITH RESISTANCE BANDS

3 SETS OF 10-12 REPS

Strong shoulders are important for endurance in throwing or swinging. Think of a softball pitcher whipping her arm windmill-style over and over throughout a seven-inning game. Will she still have the stamina to throw that nasty rise ball for a strikeout in the final inning? What about the tennis player in a third-set tiebreaker? Will she be able to smash an overhead for the win?

WHAT YOU'LL NEED

- resistance bands
- stability ball (optional)

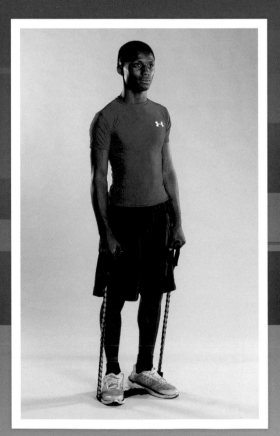

1. Hold down the middle of the resistance band with your feet, standing shoulder-width apart.

2. Hold the ends of the band in each hand.

3. Bend your elbows at 90-degree angles, and put your hands up at head level (you should look like a football goalpost). Keep your wrists straight, and make sure there is no slack in the band.

4. Raise your arms straight over your head.

5. Bring your arms back to the original position.

VARIATION

THE OVERHEAD PRESS CAN ALSO BE DONE WHILE SITTING ON A STABILITY BALL. PUT THE BAND UNDER THE BALL TO HOLD IT DOWN. KEEP YOUR BACK STRAIGHT AND YOUR KNEES BENT.

Trunk, Back, and Abs

Pavel Datsyuk of the Detroit Red Wings is considered one of the best two-way forwards in the National Hockey League. He won the NHL's Selke Trophy three times in a row. He was honored for his amazing ability to play at a high level at both ends of the ice. He helped the offense score goals and played strong defense. To be a good two-way player, you have to be able to do everything well. That includes shooting and passing, skating, checking, hitting, and defending. It also means you get a lot of ice time.

All players who reach the NHL need a strong core. Abdominals and muscles in your abdomen, sides, and lower back are used in almost everything you do. They make up the center of your power and balance. NHL players need a strong core to survive a long season playing one of the most physically demanding sports.

Having a strong core benefits your stamina for all sports. The force created by your legs transfers to the upper body through the core. That force is used by golfers, track-and-field throwers, tennis players, and volleyball players. If your core is weak, the force is lost, fatigue sets in faster, and endurance is lost.

Core for Endurance Sports

Although endurance sports have been separated from other sports in this book, one area of training that's important to all sports is core strength. Your core holds up your upper body. For a long-distance runner, proper posture is important for efficient running and more stamina. A weak core can cause your posture to slip. Poor technique will slow you down and wear you out.

NHL CENTER
PAVEL DATSYUK

ABDOMINALS—MUSCLES BELOW THE CHEST IN THE
    STOMACH AREA
POSTURE—POSITION OF YOUR BODY

MEDICINE BALL PUSH-UPS

15 REPS

One of the simplest exercises you can do to build endurance in your upper body is the reliable push-up. By adding a medicine ball to the exercise, you can get a super core workout as well. This is a drill that can benefit athletes in all sports, including distance runners.

WHAT YOU'LL NEED

- medicine ball
- exercise mat (optional)

1. Start on your knees with your legs crossed at the ankles and both hands on the medicine ball.

2. Lower your chest down to the ball and push back up.

3. Move your right hand to the floor and keep your left hand on the ball. Do another push-up.

4. Move your right hand back to the ball and put your left hand on the floor. Do another push-up.

The Importance of Breathing

Breathing is an involuntary action. You don't have to remember to breathe as you walk to school, eat, or talk to your friends. But when you exercise, it helps to concentrate on breathing. Make sure your body and muscles are getting enough oxygen. Breathe in and out during each of your drills.

CRUNCHES

1 OR 2 SETS OF 15-20 REPS

Like push-ups, sit-up crunches are an old, reliable exercise. But they still get the job done when it comes to strengthening your abs and other core muscles. Find out how many you can do and try to improve on that number throughout your training. As your stamina for crunches grows, your stamina for your sport likely will too.

> ## WHAT YOU'LL NEED
>
> • floor mat (optional)

1. Lie on your back with your knees bent up and your hands behind your head.

2. Curl your upper body forward, barely lifting your shoulders off the floor.

3. Hold for one second before returning to the floor. Count how many you can do before needing a break.

VARIATION

YOU CAN WORK YOUR OBLIQUES BY DOING CRUNCHES WITH A TWIST. WHEN YOU SIT UP, ROTATE YOUR SHOULDERS SO THAT YOUR RIGHT ELBOW POINTS AT YOUR LEFT KNEE. THE NEXT TIME ROTATE YOUR SHOULDERS SO THAT YOUR LEFT ELBOW POINTS TO YOUR RIGHT KNEE. YOU CAN DO A SET OF EACH SIDE OR ALTERNATE TWISTS WITH EACH CRUNCH.

SUPERHERO

3 SETS OF 10-20 REPS – – – – – – – – – – – –

You might not have the powers of a superhero, but you'll feel like one as you build your endurance with this exercise. Pretend to fly like a superhero while lying on the floor as you strengthen core muscles and the muscles in your lower back.

WHAT YOU'LL NEED

- floor mat (optional)
- small pillow or rolled towels (optional)

1. Lie on your stomach face down. Use a pillow or towel for support under your waist and for comfort under your head.

2. Hold your arms out above your head so that you look like you're flying.

3. Raise your arms and legs off the floor. Hold for three seconds.

4. Lower your arms and legs to the floor.

VARIATION

INSTEAD OF LIFTING ALL FOUR LIMBS OFF THE FLOOR AT ONCE, TRY TAKING TURNS WITH EACH ARM AND LEG. YOU CAN ALSO DO THE SUPERHERO BY LIFTING YOUR LEFT ARM AND RIGHT LEG TOGETHER, FOLLOWED BY YOUR RIGHT ARM AND LEFT LEG.

MEDICINE BALL TWISTS

3 SETS OF 10 REPS

Medicine balls add weight and resistance to your workout and help build muscles along the way. When you notice your endurance improve, add more reps or trade lighter balls for heavier ones. In this drill, twist your body in the same way you would when throwing a ball or swinging a golf club.

WHAT YOU'LL NEED

- medicine ball

1. Sit on the floor with your knees bent and your feet slightly raised.

2. Lean backward so your back is at a 45-degree angle with the floor. Hold the medicine ball in front of you.

3. Twist your torso slowly to the right and touch the ball to the floor beside you.

4. Twist to your left side and touch the ball to the floor beside you. Touching down on both sides is one rep.

It's Not a Race

In all of your workouts, remember: Quality is more important than quantity. Don't rush yourself through your drills. Focus on proper technique, whether it's your running style, arm angles, or posture. Doing 10 push-ups or crunches correctly is better than doing 20 incorrectly.

Repair and Rebuild

Just as each of the exercises have breaks built in for rest and recovery, it's equally important to have full days for rest. Training hard every single day of the week can be bad for you. It can make you feel weak or make you prone to injuries. Your body needs time to repair and rebuild sore muscles and to strengthen those areas you've worked so hard to train.

Elite athletes might use their rest days to relax their muscles in a hot tub or get a massage. If you don't have those opportunities, you shouldn't do "nothing" on your rest day. Go for a walk or a light bike ride. You could even do some stretching exercises. Stay active—just don't overdo it!

Take Care of Yourself!

Throughout your training be sure you're getting proper sleep, eating healthy, and drinking plenty of fluids.

U.S. OLYMPIC SOCCER GOALIE HOPE SOLO

NFL QUARTERBACK
AARON RODGERS

Stamina doesn't come naturally for athletes. It takes practice to win races like Usain Bolt and guard the net like Hope Solo. Hard work and patience will help close out fourth quarters like Silvia Fowles and Aaron Rodgers. You need determination to survive games and matches like Duncan Keith and Serena Williams. So work hard, but have fun too!

Glossary

abdominals—the muscles below the chest in the stomach area; also called abs

aerobic—with oxygen

anaerobic—without oxygen

efficiency—getting the most out of a workout with the least amount of energy used

elastic—able to change by stretching or squeezing and return to original shape

endurance—ability to keep doing an activity for a long period of time

fatigue—state of being very tired

hydrate—to achieve a healthy balance of fluids in the body

interval—the space or time between two points

medicine ball—weighted ball used for training and exercise; also called an exercise ball

obliques—side abdominal muscles that help you bend and rotate your torso

plyometrics—high-intensity workouts that focus on explosive muscle movements; also known as plyos

posture—position of your body

ratio—two numbers that are compared to each other

repetitions—the number of times an exercise is done in a set; also called reps

stamina—the energy and strength to do something for a long time

technique—way or method of doing something that requires skill

velocity—measure of an object's speed and direction

Read More

Lancaster, Scott, and Radu Teodorescu. *Athletic Fitness for Kids.* Champaign, Ill.: Human Kinetics, 2008.

Mason, Paul. *Improving Endurance.* New York: PowerKids Press, 2011.

Pire, Neal. *Plyometrics for Athletes of All Levels: Exercises in Explosive Speed and Power.* Berkeley, Calif.: Ulysses Press, 2006.

Internet Sites

FactHound offers a safe, fun way to find Internet sites related to this book. All of the sites on FactHound have been researched by our staff.

Here's all you do:

Visit *www.facthound.com*

Type in this code: 9781429676793

Index